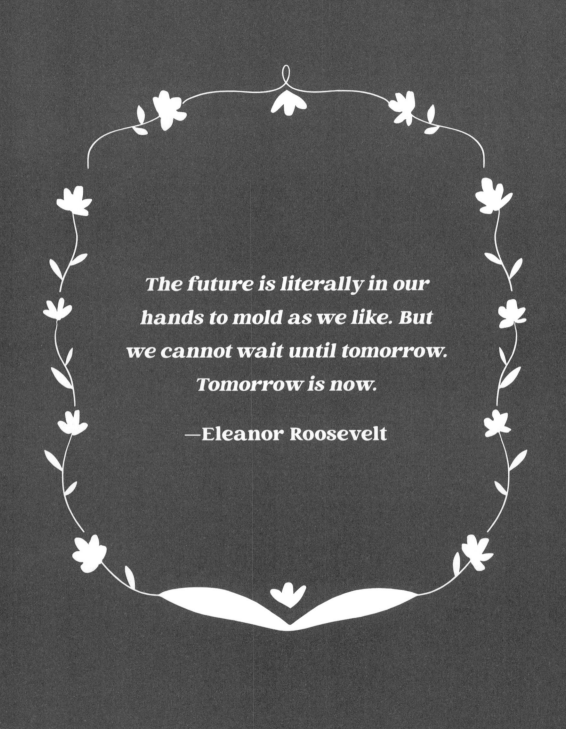

The future is literally in our hands to mold as we like. But we cannot wait until tomorrow. Tomorrow is now.

—Eleanor Roosevelt

ELEANOR ROOSEVELT

Her Path to Kindness

Helaine Becker

Illustrated by **Aura Lewis**

Christy Ottaviano Books

Little, Brown and Company
New York Boston

Eleanor had always felt at home in
her father's arms. Safe.

But now the fog clotted around them.
Where had the waves gone? The sky?

THUMP!

The SS *Britannic* was taking Eleanor and her family
from New York to England when it was rammed by
another ocean liner. The captain feared it might sink.
They had to abandon ship!

The lifeboat, far below, pitched and yawed.

Father raised his arms. "Jump!" he yelled.
But he looked so small. Eleanor . . . just . . . couldn't!

In an effort to save her, a crewman
threw Eleanor overboard into the lifeboat.
She plunged, screaming, down to the sea.

Eleanor survived the ordeal, but the
experience was never forgotten.

As time passed, Eleanor's fears swelled and multiplied.

She was afraid of
        mice,
          snakes,
            and horses.
               She was afraid of the dark.

She was even afraid of other children.

Then tragedy struck. Eleanor's mother, brother, and father died, all within two years. Eleanor was sent to live with Grandmother Hall.

There was not much kindness in Grandmother Hall's house.

Eleanor felt more frightened
and lonely than ever.

When Eleanor was fifteen, Grandmother Hall wrote a letter to Allenswood, a girls' boarding school in England. Without consulting Eleanor, she asked if they would take her granddaughter in.

The school said yes.

The headmistress of Allenswood had a penetrating gaze. As she considered young Eleanor, Mademoiselle Souvestre's eyes softened. She thought that this sad, shy girl had something special to offer.

Mademoiselle Souvestre took Eleanor under her wing.
She called Eleanor "Totty." And Eleanor was allowed to call
Mademoiselle Souvestre "Sou."

Under Sou's guidance, Eleanor began to come out of her shell.

Eleanor was able to help girls who struggled with their lessons.

She rushed to comfort those who seemed lonely or sad.

She participated in sports, even when she didn't want to. She worked hard and improved so much that she eventually made the varsity field hockey team.

The other girls grew to admire Eleanor. Every Saturday, they'd leave violets in her room as their way of saying "Thank you" and "We love you."

At Allenswood, Eleanor found her first true home. She was no longer lonely. And for the first time in her life, she was not afraid.

Meanwhile, Sou had plans for Eleanor.
She invited her on a trip to the Continent.

"You'll organize everything," Sou said. "You'll do the packing and unpacking, arrange the schedules, buy the tickets, and read all the maps."

Eleanor jumped at the chance. She loved the responsibility and the freedom of doing things for herself.

On the train to Pisa, the conductor called out
the name of a town by the sea.

Sou's eyes sparkled. "I've always enjoyed seeing the stars shine
over the Mediterranean. I'm sure you will too." She tossed her
suitcase off the train and jumped out! So did Eleanor.

It was the greatest thrill of Eleanor's young life.

Eleanor spent three glorious years at Allenswood. But she knew she would have to return to New York before her final year. Grandmother Hall expected Eleanor to "debut" in high society and find a suitable husband.

Eleanor would never forget Mademoiselle Souvestre. Sou had given her a home. But more importantly, she'd taught Eleanor how to make a home for herself—inside her own heart.

Eleanor wasn't the least bit interested in becoming a debutante. So while she went along with her grandmother's wishes, she also joined a new charitable organization called the Junior League. With another league volunteer, she'd teach at the College Settlement on Rivington Street, a community center that catered to recent immigrants.

As she approached the settlement house for the first time, a wave of terror threatened to engulf her. What poverty!

But Eleanor resolved not to let
her old enemy, fear, get the better of her.

Instead, she jumped in with both feet—literally!

Her job was teaching children
exercises and dance.

Sincerely yours,
Eleanor Roosevelt

Eleanor also became an investigator for the Consumers' League of New York City. In that role, she visited sweatshops where children as young as four made artificial flowers in overcrowded garrets. Appalled by what she saw, Eleanor wrote open letters to newspapers, advocating for better working conditions.

In the tenements of New York, surrounded by friends and doing work she loved, Eleanor was finally in her element. She had no time for fear—her work was too important!

Toot! Toot!

Eleanor's mind and heart were full as the train pulled into the station. She had so much to tell Grandmother Hall when she arrived at their country house on the Hudson. To her surprise, she bumped into her cousin Franklin, on his way to his own country home.

Throwing caution to the wind, Eleanor told Franklin about her grand plans to make the world a better place: one without poverty, where people could improve their lives through better health care, education, and regulated working conditions.

Franklin got a twinkle in his eye.
"That is a wonderful idea," he agreed.

With Franklin's backing, Eleanor embarked on a thrilling new adventure—to make her sweeping vision a reality. Now that she'd managed to overcome her fears, she'd let nothing stand in her way.

Eleanor's warm heart, devotion to hard work, and belief in public service inspired many others to join her. Together, they would take action. Together, they would change the world.

*Courage is more exhilarating than fear
and in the long run it is easier.*

—Eleanor Roosevelt

The fundamental basis of good behavior in kindness and consideration for others has never changed.

—Eleanor Roosevelt

AUTHOR'S NOTE

Anna Eleanor Roosevelt was born in 1884 into one of the wealthiest, best-known families in America. But her early life was not a charmed or happy one. Eleanor's mother was a frivolous high-society beauty, who called Eleanor "Granny" and made her feel unattractive. Eleanor's father, who grappled with substance abuse, behaved erratically. He was known to shower "Little Nell" with affection and then callously neglect her. With little parental oversight, Eleanor was raised by a stern nanny. She'd pull Eleanor's hair when she braided it and assign harsh punishments for minor mistakes, like sloppy sewing.

When Eleanor was two and a half years old, while traveling with her family from New York to England, their ship, the SS *Britannic*, collided with the SS *Celtic*. Lifeboats began to transfer passengers from the *Britannic* to the *Celtic* before the crew determined the ship would not sink. The trauma left Eleanor with prolonged anxiety. She became so timid that she sometimes refused to play with other children.

Eleanor's mother, brother, and father all died before she turned ten. In the wake of these tragedies, Eleanor and her baby brother, Hall, went to live with their grandmother, Mary Livingston Ludlow Hall.

Grandmother Hall was as emotionally neglectful as Eleanor's parents were. She provided the necessities of life but without outward affection. Instead, she raised Eleanor in a spartan environment, shuttling between homes in New York City and Tivoli, New York. Neither house offered warmth or comfort. Eleanor later confessed to her Aunt Corinne, "Auntie, I have no real home."

Another of her aunts, Auntie Bye, helped fifteen-year-old Eleanor escape her grandmother's rigid rules. She urged Grandmother Hall to send Eleanor to a school in England that she'd attended herself.

Allenswood was unusually progressive. It was run by an imposing French headmistress, Mademoiselle

Marie Souvestre, who believed in teaching students the skills and confidence they'd need to change the world. Eleanor later wrote that Souvestre "shocked me into thinking, and that on the whole was very beneficial." Souvestre also gave Eleanor the unshakable belief that "the underdog was always the one to be championed."

At Allenswood, Eleanor flourished. She felt seen, understood, and cared for there. She established deep friendships with Souvestre and her classmates. She learned how to step into the limelight, without letting fear hold her back.

You must do the thing
you think you cannot do.
—Eleanor Roosevelt

Eleanor had one year remaining at Allenswood when she had to leave—she was expected back in New York. Grandmother Hall insisted Eleanor become a debutante when she turned eighteen. She would be displayed to potential husbands at an endless round of parties and dances. Eleanor found the situation "utter agony."

A glimmer of light came when she joined the Junior League for the Promotion of Settlement Movements in 1903. The organization was founded in 1901 by Eleanor's acquaintances, two wealthy, well-educated young women who wanted to make a difference.

As a volunteer at the College Settlement on Riv-ington Street, Eleanor discovered a sense of purpose. Through social action, she could do as her beloved Mademoiselle Souvestre urged: change the world.

Eleanor's experiences on New York's Lower East Side were eye-opening. She saw firsthand the squalor where recent immigrants, mostly Jews from Eastern Europe, had to live and work. The settlement house gave them practical support and offered a pathway out of the slums through education and self-improvement. Eleanor later said that her work there and at the Consumers' League of New York City made her grow up. It showed her a world she otherwise might never have imagined.

Shortly after she'd returned from Allenswood, Eleanor bumped into her distant cousin Franklin Delano Roosevelt on a train to Tivoli. They were both heading to their respective family country houses along the Hudson River. While we don't know exactly what the pair discussed during the trip, she may have told him about her commitment to help others. Franklin was fascinated by Eleanor and her opinions. After an extended engagement, the pair married in 1905.

Justice cannot be for one side alone,
but must be for both.
—Eleanor Roosevelt

Over the next few decades, Franklin Delano Roosevelt took on increasingly more important political posts. Ultimately, he became president of the United States. With Eleanor's help and inspiration, he instituted groundbreaking policies to help the elderly, the ill, and the very poor. His New Deal programs included the establishment of Social Security and the Works Progress Administration.

You gain strength, courage, and confidence by every experience in which you really stop to look fear in the face. You are able to say to yourself, "I lived through this horror. I can take the next thing that comes along."

—Eleanor Roosevelt

Eleanor, meanwhile, worked tirelessly for civil rights and social justice. As First Lady, she shared her views widely in a daily newspaper column, weekly radio shows, and a monthly magazine column.

She later became a member of the first US delegation to the United Nations, the first chair of the UN Commission on Human Rights, and the chair of the President's Commission on the Status of Women.

I shall never cease to hope that I may awaken in others a sense of the importance of these nations to the future of the world and a realization that we have strong potential friends there.

—Eleanor Roosevelt

Eleanor was, perhaps most notably, the driving force behind the historic Universal Declaration of Human Rights. That document set out basic rights for people everywhere, regardless of race, age, or gender—*for the first time in history*. Adopted in 1948, the declaration continues to influence international law today.

We all create the person we become by our choices as we go through life. In a very real sense, by the time we are adult, we are the sum total of the choices we have made.

—Eleanor Roosevelt

REFERENCES AND FURTHER RESOURCES

- Cooney, Barbara. *Eleanor*. Viking, 1996.
- Gerber, Robin. *Leadership the Eleanor Roosevelt Way*. Prentice Hall, 2002.
- Jacobs, William Jay. *Eleanor Roosevelt: A Life of Happiness and Tears*. Coward-McCann, 1983.
- MacLeod, Elizabeth. *Eleanor Roosevelt: An Inspiring Life*. Kids Can Press, 2006.
- Muñoz Ryan, Pam, and Brian Selznick, illustrator. *Amelia and Eleanor Go for a Ride*. Scholastic, 1999.
- Rappaport, Doreen, and Gary Kelley, illustrator. *Eleanor, Quiet No More*. Hyperion, 2009.
- Roosevelt, Eleanor. *The Moral Basis of Democracy*. Open Road, 1940.